DOGGERLAND

By the same author

Black Tulips
The Wardrobe

DOGGERLAND

MOYA PACEY

RECENT
WORK
PRESS

Doggerland
Recent Work Press
Canberra, Australia

Copyright © Moya Pacey, 2020

ISBN: 9780648834397 (paperback)

 A catalogue record for this book is available from the National Library of Australia

All rights reserved. This book is copyright. Except for private study, research, criticism or reviews as permitted under the Copyright Act, no part of this book may be reproduced, stored in a retrieval system, or transmitted in any form by any means without prior written permission. Enquiries should be addressed to the publisher.

Cover image: Original painting © Martina Penning mrhanki71@gmail.com 'Tent' illustration by John Brady whitbyjb@netspeed.com.au both reproduced with permission.

Cover design: Recent Work Press
Set by Recent Work Press

recentworkpress.com

MD

For my family

'Home-made, home-made! But aren't we all?'

Elizabeth Bishop from *Crusoe in England*

Contents

Doggerland	1
Gardener	2
Your Dad Talks Funny	3
My Brothers and My Sister	4
I Feel You Breathing	5
Egging	6
Birders	7
Street Games	8
At the Circus	9
Food Talk	10
Fractions	11
The Interview	12
People on the Tele Are Not Like Us	14
Wintering	15
Missing	16
Everything Goes Together	17
Everything Feels Right	18
The Queen Mother	19
Grandfather Jack	20
Lost Souls	21
Father Christmas and Our Chimney	22
At the Children's Library	23
The Cuban Missile Crisis 1962	25
This Is What Happens	26
Wallflowers	28
He Can Dance and He Can Sing	29
She Can['t] Play the Violin	31
Park	32
Swans Know How	33
Home is a Feather	35
Murder by Person or Persons Unknown	36
Safe Seat	37
Disney Princess	38
The Girl Who Said No	39

In the Schoolroom	40
When I Draw My Life	41
Answer the Door	42
Party circa 1966	43
In the Photograph, My Mother Wears a Shirtwaister	44
Rearranging the Furniture	45
Tent	46
Deserter	48
I Dream My Father	49
You're Never Far Away	50
Glimpse	51
The Intellectual	52
Untitled	54
War Coat	55
Ice House	56
Afterword	57

Doggerland

Most times it's winter. White as bandages. Red with scarlet fever. Two men wearing peaked caps appear on the road, driving a cream coloured ambulance. When I see them stop a few doors down, I hold my collar until I see a dog for luck. So do the other kids. The ambulance men carry out the taxi driver's daughter, Josie, on a stretcher. We never see her again.

My friend's father vanishes every few months into the Merchant Navy. After he's gone, she stops holding her breath, smooths her rainbow skin and comes outside to play...

Our neighbour, the soldier deserter, breaks through from his house into our attic and hides. He gives his wife a black eye and breaks her nose. The Military Police wearing red caps drag him down our stairs. Mam scrubs and scrubs until the blood goes.

Across the road, a baby boy called Paul burned in a Moses cradle. Growing up, he has a hook for a hand. Half his face ruined. One eye. He chases me across the street ready to strike. I manage to open the front door of my house, slip inside, slam it in his face and disappear. His hook gouges out a chunk of wood in our red front door.

Two boys from my class chase me home from school. One of them called Anthony has hands that are always wet. I am a fast runner and think I've lost them. I hide in the library but when I come out, they're still there. The boys always leave where their street turns away from mine.

Dad grows our food: potatoes, onions, spinach and cabbages. Dad does not roam. He never leaves us like the other fathers who go out their back doors shouting they're going for cigarettes and never come home.

Gardener

Evenings after work, Dad's
in our garden turning
thin soil with a spade.
Sleeves of his woolly jumper
pushed high, past bony elbows.
Dad's foot pauses on the rim
of the blade, shakes out a cigarette
from the packet in his pocket.
Mam comes out of the house,
an unlit cigarette held
between red lips.
Dad's fingers fumble,
                      strike a match.

Your Dad Talks Funny

he does not

he does and his name's Paddy

he does not and his name's not Paddy

it's Charlie Brady

When Dad comes home from work, he tells me he dropped his keys in a pine wood. 'I was all the way back at the van when I realised they were gone. I went back into the wood to search, saying a prayer to St Anthony and found them at my feet. If you lose something special, Moya, say a prayer to St Anthony.'

I listen hard to his soft words.

His voice is my Dad's voice.
Not Paddy's.

My Brothers and My Sister

John is my best friend. He keeps his soldiers in a biscuit tin with a castle on the front and green and blue glass marbles in his trouser pockets. He gives me one called a 'tiger's eye' to mind. He never hits and some of his hair won't lie down at the top. My big brother got the scissors one day and cut it off.

Judy sings on the stairs, in her bed, and at the tea table. She swings her skinny legs and sings, and sings. Her favourite is, 'Seven little girls, sitting in the back seat, kissing and a hugging with Fred.'

On Friday, we got a new baby brother. Aunt Lily came down stairs and told us his hair was black. At school, I finished my card for the black babies in Africa and Miss Carolyn said, 'Now, you can choose a name for him or her.' I chose a boy baby. I called him, Peter.

I Feel You Breathing

for Peter

Mam puts you into the cradle
I've made for you with my arms.
I trace the flower petals, raised
blues and greens stitched on the blanket
Mam made to swaddle you tight.
I take you to the window, push
aside the winter night curtain, 'Careful
don't drop him', Mam calls.
I won't drop you. I'm showing you our world.
Look!
Shadows, smelly smoke, chimney-pots,
street lamps yellow with sodium light.
There's the snow slide we made,
shining like the Milky Way. Your eyes
two blue perfect moons
meet mine in one long stare.

I know this place. I know you. You don't need to say.

Egging

Boys like my brothers steal eggs.
Climb trees, stopping at high branches
poke fingers into warm nests
peering into crevices
in crumbling stone walls or
any hole that looks promising.
They part hawthorn bushes, red
with berries, careless of thorns ripping
through sleeves of soft woollen jumpers.
Arms outstretched, fingers and thumbs
feeling for eggs. Boys like my brothers
at the end of the long day, broken
fingernails, bloody hands. Each boy
cradles a prize in his palm,
not trusting trouser pockets.
Brings it home to blow
goodness and life gently out.
Careful not to crack the blue
speckled, silent shell.
It joins others on the window sill
in the back kitchen, next to a sliver
of green soap and a comb
with broken teeth.

Birders

Instead of smelting steel or driving
forklifts at the port, men are buying bird
books, spotting, making blogs, competing.
Last week, Pete scored a willow warbler.
Harry beat that with an orange-breasted
whinchat. Wildlife Centres springing
up where smokestacks once belched
hot air and muck. Dads and granddads
walking lads out over marsh,
telling tales of birds' long journeys.
Places where they fed, watered,
rested in sanctuaries now disappeared.

In the hide, men whisper names—
shoveler, pochard, lapwing,
redshank—once a glossy ibis.
The lads are their apprentices.
Men help them to adjust the lenses
of binoculars, so that when
they close one eye and squint,
they see
the world changed
        for birds and men.

Street Games

Thud.

I throw two red balls
at the brick wall of our house.

Thud.

Charlie Chaplin went to France
To show the ladies how to dance
First you do the rhumba
Then you do the kicks
Then you do the turn around
Then you do the splits

Thud.

Dad's planting spuds.
I join the girls out on the street at the skipping rope.

Eva Weaver, Chimney Sweeper
Had a wife but couldn't keep her
Had another didn't love her
Up the chimney he did shove her

Someone's Mam shouts, 'Tea's ready.'

One, two, three
The rope drops. Everyone goes
home. I drift off, not wanting
to leave the game, and the street
goes straight past our house and three lamp posts
until it runs out of its name.

At the Circus

Don't let the clowns choose me to go into the ring. They pretend to throw buckets of water but they're paper stars. Gold and silver stars glittering. I don't want everyone staring. I don't like clown faces. The one with the pointed hat has round, hard eyes like the steel ball bearings my brother plays marbles with. He smashes glass ones when he fires them hard. There are gaps in the wooden slats under my seat. I am keeping my legs straight together and my feet neat because my brother says underneath is where the lions are waiting to go into the ring. I smell their smell and hear their roars.

Elephants have kind eyes. Small and soft not like the eyes of the clown with the pointy hat. Elephants watch each other and walk in a line hooking their trunk on to the one in front's tail. Making a circle around the ringmaster so they don't have to be whipped. They are careful stepping in case they step on a mouse. They are scared of mice like I am scared of lions. The stars on their heads crease like my bed sheet when I've slept on it too long and their skin wrinkles. They are old elephants.

I can't see the eyes on the face of the girl on the trapeze. She's too far away. Her partner is putting something on his hands so they won't slip when he catches her. She swings and swings and then she leaves go and throws herself at him. I peep through my fingers. She's caught but one day she will fall, I know, into the net below. One day I will fall between the slats beneath my seat and the lions will be there.

Food Talk

Fruit falls from the pear tree
or comes in a brown paper bag—
a Fyffes banana from Jamaica
or an orange from somewhere hot.
Meat and two veg for school dinner.
Heinz beans at home on toast
for tea with eggs from Josie's hens.
For supper we look in the pantry
for something to put in a sandwich.
Sunday nights—bubble and squeak.
Sometimes there's mousetrap—
hard red cheese. Mam says,
eating cheese late at night
means 'You'll see your dead Grannie.'
Mine's not dead.

Fractions

for Jonathan

i/ a numerical quantity that is not a whole number; ii/ a small or tiny part, amount, or proportion of something.

When I couldn't get the hang
of fractions—
Dad bought a cake
sliced it
This is a half
Sliced it again
This is a quarter
Sliced it again
This is an eighth
And half of an eighth
what would that be?
I wasn't sure
Dad cut the eighth in half
This is $1/16^{th}$
Here is $1/32^{nd}$
And a half of that is?
Dad couldn't stop himself
cutting and slicing
the numbers getting higher
higher, but the fractions
smaller and smaller
tinier and tinier
until nothing was left
of cake but crumbs
I like cake
I don't like sums

The Interview

When I was eleven years old, I nearly passed the scholarship exam except first, I had to go to the convent and have an interview before they'd let me go there. I practised and practised at school some of the questions I might get asked, then I went around to a girl's house who'd passed the interview the year before and she told me to remember to count how many steps there were on the way from the front door of the convent to the room where I would be interviewed. It was really important, she said. On the day of the interview, I counted all the steps and hoped I'd remember when they asked me. Inside the room, were three people sitting at a big shiny table. I had to sit facing them all. There was a nun called Reverend Mother, an old lady wearing a brown hat and a big man wearing a suit and tie.

Reverend Mother asked what book I was reading and when I said 'Heidi' the big man sitting at the table asked me in a very loud voice, Did I know what country Heidi lived in?

I said I did. The old lady wearing a brown hat said, 'What country is that?'

I said Switzerland.

Then the man said, 'Let's imagine you are going to Switzerland from Middlesbrough. Now then. How would you get there?'

Well, first I would go to the train station and get on a train to London but I would need to buy a ticket and I'm not sure how much it costs to go there because I have never been. I have been on a train to Whitby for my holiday and my Dad had to save up for all our fares.

'Don't worry about that,' said the man.

I was worried about that but I didn't say.

'Where would you go after London?' the man said.

After London, I would have to get on a boat and that will be expensive, but I'm not sure because I have never been on a boat except for the row boat on Albert Park Lake and the boat that goes around Whitby harbour on my holiday.

'Where will the boat take you?' asked the man.

I think, I said, it might take me to France.

'Aren't you sure?' asked the old lady in the brown hat.

I said, No I wasn't sure, but I had seen France in an atlas but I had never been there in my life.

'You are correct,' said the big man. 'The boat is called a ferry and it will take you to France and after France, where then?'

I said I didn't know.

I wanted them to ask how many steps I had climbed to get to them all in that dark room at the top of the stairs in the convent. There were a lot of steps. And I remembered how many.

They never asked.

People on the Tele Are Not Like Us

They have names like Lady Isabel and Sir Gilbert and live in London and dress as if they're going out somewhere very special. They talk a lot but not like us. They don't say 'swilling' or 'nithered' and no-one says, 'I'll put the kettle on.'

They don't go outside very much. If they do, they don't catch a bus. A man drives them where they want to go. Sometimes they go into their kitchens. There are no plates on the table or any washing up in the sink and when they open a cupboard, nothing falls out. They go in there to tell Cook what they want to eat that night.

We don't see their children. They are upstairs in the nursery with someone called Nanny.

In my house when we switch off the tele—we are all together—Mam and Dad and my whole family—we've had our supper and now it's time for bed.

Dad dampens down the fire—we say good night and go up the stairs taking turns to use the bathroom—Dad comes up last and turns out the light.

Wintering

Dad's in the kitchen: turning on taps,
knocking crockery, banging saucepans,
clicking cupboard doors shut.
Chris is in the cherry-red rocking chair
watching an episode of *The Fugitive*.
John and Judy play a dumb show,
stifle giggles because baby's asleep
bottle fallen from his hand. Milk
pools in the cracks of the leather sofa
drips on to the green carpet.

The coal fire settles to a garnet of heat.
Outside, the road shadowed in sodium light.
Snow lays fast.
Tomorrow we'll make long slides
Annoy the neighbours.
Tonight, the shivery bark of a neighbour's dog
Wanting to be let in.

Missing

I think my mother went away. I am at my bedroom window with my brothers. Mine is the smallest bedroom in the house, with a window, looking out over the road. So, if she comes home, we will see her. But we've looked and looked and she isn't there. We are dressed in our night clothes, either getting ready for bed, or we've been woken up to get ready for her coming home. A stretch of shadowy grass in the half-light. Street lights shine down on the empty road. No mother.

Mr and Mrs Nenius live across the road. Their lights are on. Mr Nenius is from Lithuania. He doesn't go to work and stays in his house. Mrs Nenius is from Wales. We don't understand what she says. Mam says people from Wales can sing very well but I've never heard Mrs Nenius sing. Mr Nenius is very sick and dying slowly in his own front bedroom. He can't be saved. All we can do is pray for him. My Dad sits with him most nights and they pray the Rosary together. I should feel safe but I don't. We are waiting for our mother and she hasn't come yet.

Everything Goes Together

On Sundays, I go to morning Mass and sometimes in the afternoon to Benediction. My friend Sandra goes to Sunday School because she goes to a different church. I've never been there. I don't want to.

I like Benediction. I like the way everything goes together. The smell of the incense floating up and swirling like a good cloud. I take my glasses off and the colours of flowers on the altar mix together. Like a painting. Best of all is the music. It's in Latin. I can't speak it. I close my eyes. Some of it is sad.

The priest uses two hands to lift the gold monstrance. It flashes like the sun. When he puts it back down, it's very quiet. He wipes it carefully before he locks it away in the tabernacle, then smooths the altar cloths and folds them in a special way. He doesn't hurry and he knows where everything goes because he's done it over and over. Everything he touches is very holy.

Benediction is always the same.

On the way home, I meet Sandra, 'I drew a picture of Jesus', she says,

'What did you do?'

Everything Feels Right

I am going there again. Slipping through the gate to find the place we're not allowed where everything feels right. It's behind a hedge that scratches and you have to know the place to squeeze through and we do. I go with my brother not on my own. There's a long pool you can walk around and look down into water. We don't touch anything not even the water. We just look at the big white flowers floating like soft stars. We don't know how they float like that.

It's dark where the pool is but the light gets in sometimes through the slats above our heads. We walk in the dark and the light lets us see fish gliding swimming weaving in and out beneath the surface. We don't catch them. They are silver and gold and bigger than the goldfish that swim in the glass bowl on our sideboard. We look for a long time. Some kids might throw a stone into the pool but we never do. And we don't say anything because it's quiet.

The Queen Mother

The only Queen Mother we know is our Nana, at least that's what Dad calls her, but there is another one and she lives in a castle.

That Queen Mother doesn't open her own curtains. They must be very heavy. Someone else squeezes toothpaste on to her brush. Our curtains are easy to open and our toothpaste comes in a tin with a lid that sticks.

The Queen Mother fishes in a river for salmon. We look for tadpoles in the beck and put them in a jam-jar full of beck water and watch them swarm but we never get a frog.

The Queen Mother wears a tartan kilt like I do with a big safety pin.

She has gardens everywhere and gardeners pushing wheelbarrows. We have our Dad digging spuds and cabbages and trying to get his onions to grow.

The Queen Mother loves horses. We have the rag and bone man come with his horse and cart. He shouts 'Any old iron?' and we look in our wash house for something to give him. He likes anything made of metal and will swap you for an orange goldfish in a plastic bag filled with water.

The Queen Mother likes games especially the Highland Games in Scotland. I have hockey at school in winter near the crematorium and my fingers get frozen and my ankles get banged when we bully-off.

I've seen a picture of the Queen Mother and Dad's right she is like our Nana. She's not very tall and plump and has small feet like our Nana and her hair's the same and she likes hats. So does my Nana. She lets me try them on when I go to see her.

My Nana hasn't got a castle. She lives in a house in West Crescent. It's a nice house with a black shiny piano in the front room. Her name is Margaret not Elizabeth. She curls her hair. She hasn't got a crown.

Grandfather Jack

My father's father comes to us on Good Friday wearing a long mackintosh and like a magician reaches inside poachers' pockets, bringing out rashers of bacon and half a dozen eggs. The eggs and bacon break our Lenten fast.

This never happened.

Grandfather Jack never comes to our house in England. Not once. It's Irish Uncle Tom from London who turns up at Easter wearing the 'mac, pockets full of eggs and bacon.

Not Grandfather Jack.

Irish Uncle Joe visits from Manchester, wearing a flecked tweed cap and a three-piece suit. One of his legs shorter than the other. He wears a special boot. It squeaks. My big brother, says he screws off his wooden leg each night. It gives us all bad dreams. It's not true. Uncle Joe is kind and buys ice creams and likes his photograph taken at the sea-side.

Aunty Trudy, my father's Irish sister, comes from London bringing chocolates, bottles of scent and treats. She's a nurse and wears dresses she makes herself and colours her hair purple.

Grandfather Jack never comes.

At Christmas, he sends a parcel of brown paper and string sealed with red wax stamped Co Derry, N. Ireland. Inside, a chicken without a head. It arrives in time to be cooked for dinner. Mam lights a cigarette, to help with the smell as she reaches inside to pull out its innards. But still she retches.

Mam says she met Grandfather Jack once when she crossed the Irish Sea with Dad after the war. Before any of us were born.

Our house is full of children now but we have room for Grandfather Jack if he ever wants to come...

Lost Souls

I bring them in one at a time by the side door of the church. First one is my Irish Grandmother, stuck in a small room in Derry, waving to my Dad who's eight-years old through a window. 'Say goodbye to your Mammy, son'.

Edel, the missionary, is next. I have her photo on a prayer card. She was very holy so I'm not sure why she hasn't got eternal rest but she's in Africa.

Then it's Josie's turn. Last time I saw her, she was on a stretcher covered in a red blanket. I touched my collar. We all did. Then men in black peaked caps pushed her into the ambulance. Drove her away.

To the wrong place.

I am sending them all to the right place.

Father Christmas and Our Chimney

When it's your turn you have to get close to the fire
and catch a draught so that it goes straight up the chimney and flies off
to Father Christmas in the North Pole wherever that is.
My list is written neatly on the strip of paper:

A doll with blonde hair
A book What Katy Did or The Secret Garden
A Cadbury's Selection Box
Monopoly
Bunty Annual

Except it gets caught in the chimney and soot
falls onto the new red carpet.
Mam is not best pleased
and you have to be good
so good to get the presents you want
and lucky.
We've already got seven years bad luck because Judy broke the dressing
table mirror
the really big one
the biggest in our house.
She was looking for her Christmas presents.
We know they come from our Mam.
She hides them under her bed.
Last Christmas, I found a red toy sewing machine.
It really worked.

At the Children's Library

The woman puts on her glasses,
tells me to hold out my hands
checks each fingernail, each palm,
before she nods and waves me through
to the children's shelves. I have two
tickets—one coloured blue for true.
The other pink for made-up.

I feel the woman watching.
I don't look round. I edge
a book out from its place.
The woman has shelved them
tight—there's not much space.
I'm careful because the notice says,
Please handle each book with respect.

I've read most of the books
I want to read in the made-up section.
All of Enid Blyton's 'Famous Five'.
Noel Streatfield's ballet books.
I don't like reading true
unless it's about a Queen or Florence Nightingale.

I'm not allowed to borrow
in the grown-up section until
I'm fourteen. That's four more years.
I don't know what to do.
Whenever something new
comes in, the woman says,
'That's not for you.
Hurry up, Hurry up.
You've had ample time to choose.'

Silence in the library at all times.
The woman says 'Shush, Shush'
very loud. 'I will not tell you again,
you'll get thrown out.'

She can take away my library card.
I don't know anyone who's been let back in.

The Cuban Missile Crisis 1962

at school they say that when the bomb goes off, we have to get under the table and our mothers must whitewash all our windows

our teacher asks us to put up our hands if we have questions

I have some but I don't say

there are six of us and the baby and we can't all sit around the table at the same time so how can we all sit underneath it?

how can we whitewash the upstairs windows when we don't have a ladder?

the window cleaner does them but it's not his week to come and how much extra will it cost and what's whitewash?

This Is What Happens

It's Sunday afternoon and she's in the wash house standing in stocking feet on the roof of the old doll's house, the one Uncle John Murphy made, and she's rocking backwards and forwards ...bored, bored, bored...

rebod rebod rebod rebod rebod rebod rebod rebod rebod rebod rebod

She's thinking about visiting the 'You can always come tomorrow' lady in Loxley Road. Yesterday, she stopped her and her best friend, Sandra, as they were coming home from the park, just as it was getting dark. She said, did they know where Loxley Road was and would they take her there? She said she'd give them both a chocolate biscuit if they did. They wanted a biscuit but didn't go with her because they were late for their teas and so the lady said, 'You can always come tomorrow.'

wormroot   moorwort   wormroot   moorwort   wormroot moorwort,

Sandra's gone out after her Sunday dinner with her Mam and Uncle Frank. He rides a motorbike with a side car for Sandra to ride in. Sandra's Mam puts both arms round Uncle Frank's waist and sits behind him on the bike. Sometimes, Uncle Frank takes her with them to the Breakwater and she shares the side car with Sandra. They sit side by side on the seat and there's room to stretch their legs right out. Feet and bottoms nearly touch the ground. Uncle Frank closes the plastic hood over their heads and they wave at everyone but they're gone before they can turn round to see if they wave back. This Sunday they left her behind.

The Loxley lady promised her a chocolate biscuit.

You can always come tomorrow

Can you always come tomorrow?

One little girl knocks on the door

One woman's head turns in the dark

One woman's heels tap-tapping on the floor

One little girl come to say hello

One woman opens wide the door and,

O

One little girl, inside she goes ...

Wallflowers

Wallflower Wallflower growing up so high
We are little children and we are going to die
Except for...
Tommy and Rosalyn
He can dance and he can sing
She can play the violin

He Can Dance and He Can Sing

The scent of her like my sister
soft eyes like my sister
sweet smile like my sister
Would you like some jam and bread?
She takes me by the hand
like my sister
Leads me to her door
sits me at her table
Here's your jam and bread
Eyes hard like marbles
not like my sister
Two slabs of bread
no butter
jam dripping
like blood
I feel sick
Eat your jam and bread
Her voice cold
Smile all gone
not like my sister
She goes into the kitchen
I leave her jam and bread
creep to the window
lift the sash
Slip through the gap
She grabs my ankle
I wriggle, wriggle
kick, kick
free
dancing
singing
home for tea
Come back Come back

I did not eat your jam and bread
If I did
I would be dead

She Can['t] Play the Violin

We walk home from school in winter dark after orchestra practice
She takes the path to the footbridge over the railway line
Next day she's missing
And the next and the next
and the week after, and the next
The teacher stops calling out her name
Before she disappears, she's the shiniest girl in the class
Shiny hair, shiny shoes, white socks, white blouse, tie
knotted neatly around her neck
When she comes back, she's wearing a white silk scarf
She points at her throat to explain why she can't speak
Her violin won't sit on top of the scarf
She unwraps the white coil slowly rolling it around her hand like a bandage
That's when I see
Two thumbprints

Park

you can play ball games but
keep off the grass

there's a tennis court but
you have to bring your own bat and ball

there are flowers but
you can't pick

there are bushes but
be careful bad people hide

you should be safe but
you are not

Swans Know How

Keep off the grass it says on the board
we don't
there's bushes to hide in
we don't
we don't want what happened to Mary to happen to us

there's a playground with swings, a slide and a tea-pot lid
if the Parky's in there, the big boys won't come
they're rough and shove us out of the way and don't wait until
we're off the slide
they push the swings we're on too high and won't stop
we can't get off

there's a lake with a little island in the middle
we get in a row boat and pay the man
he gives us a number
when our time finishes, he holds it up and we have to come in
some kids don't
they hide behind the island
the swans don't like that
it's their island
they sleep in nests at night
long white necks fitted underneath their wings

swans know how to save themselves like us
we tuck in our legs and arms, make ourselves small
so we don't get hit or punched or caught until it's time to go home
our mothers say where have you been, how many times
have I told you to come home before it gets too dark and they lock the gates?

we don't want to be locked in the park at night
we can't get to the swan island to be safe
the row boats are tied up
we can't swim like swans without making a noise

our legs and feet kick and splash and our arms come in and out of the water someone will hear and come and find us
it might be the man who hid in the bushes—the man who found Mary
he will come and find us before we can get home tuck in our heads and hide in our nests

Home is a Feather

I'm knee deep in wheat, crossing Corky's field
on my way to the cinder path that leads
nearly home. I pull off a spike, a yellow
feather. Prickly. Not like the feathers
I pick out from the corners of my bed pillow.
'Stop doing that', Mam says but I can't help it.

Each one's a tiny grey feather from a baby bird
who couldn't fly away. I place one
on the palm of my hand. Blow. Blow.
It floats on my breath until my breath runs out.
It's like the scab I have on my knee,
I keep picking and picking trying
to see pink new skin. It isn't ready
                                        bleeding at the edges.

Murder by Person or Persons Unknown

Mary, Mary, quite contrary
How does your garden grow?
With silver bells and cockle shells
And pretty maids all in a row

Blonde haired, blue-eyed Mary
Wearing her favourite flowery
Dress and red bonnet, hiding
From her sisters in the park

Mary, Mary,
Come out
Come out
Wherever you are

Safe Seat

If you're on the last bus home,
sit downstairs and look for the woman from the fish and chip shop.
'Here pet,' she calls and slides over so that you're jammed
next to the window.
You breathe in her dripping fat frying all night cod and chips smells.
Feet spilling over men's slippers.
Hands hard-veined, gripping her purse.
Face chapped red, lined. Hair permed,
a stiff helmet under a blue paisley headscarf.
The bus fogs up, men roll on climbing
upstairs to smoke. Those too drunk
fall into seats on the lower deck.
Some nod off. Others look for trouble.
Don't meet their eyes hard, beery, loud.
Look out the window, even though it's too dark to see anything.
When the woman from the fish and chip shop
readies herself to get off,
you're not safe without her.
Stand up and without a word spoken,
she finds you a safe seat. Another woman
tucks you in close to the window for the rest of the way home.
Women and girls unspoken, unrehearsed,
follow the script women give each other—
find themselves safe seats.

Disney Princess

She's scent stoppered in a glass bottle trapped
No magic tonight
Painted, polished
A present—gift-wrapped
She's scent stoppered in a glass bottle trapped

He's tracksuit and trainers
Fists clenched
Waiting to put out her light
She's scent stoppered in a glass bottle trapped
No magic tonight

The Girl Who Said No

Her name was Patricia
and one day she said
NO
to the free school milk in the glass bottle that stood
all morning in its crate in the hot summer sun
NO to the teacher
NO to the headmaster
NO NO NO
She ran from the line-up
out of the playground
out of the gate

It was the day I heard the venetian blinds rattle in the classroom
Watching each slat cutting the day into long thin slices
Blinking at patterns of dark and light
Thinking this moment might go on and on
and on and never end and I was trapped
not like Patricia and her NO

But I didn't say no
Not to warm milk
or to boys with hands that were wet
or to the man on a train who sat too close
or to the man in the car smelling of tweed

In the Schoolroom

I am counting the horizontal slats on the venetian blinds over and over. The others are writing in their feint ruled notebooks over and over solving the problem the teacher has chalked on the blackboard. Miss Carolyn stands at the front keeping guard in case we all rise suddenly, a flock of sparrows in one big flight out of the classroom, down the long corridor, out the green door on to the asphalt playground, flying over neat rows of milk bottles.

Summer heat curdles milk clotted at the necks of bottles so that when I push the glossy gum-coated paper straw through the silver cap, I have to poke until it reaches the liquid of what's left of milk. The smell of it catches in the back of my throat. A smell I could cut with a pocket knife if I had one.

>my seven-year old fingers

>tracing the wooden desk

>pattern long gone

When I Draw My Life

The sun a circle of cadmium yellow.
Seven curved lines veer off

anti-clockwise, rays to warm
the square house below.

Four windows—two up
two down—either side of the closed door.

Six tall tulips shaded hard in magenta
inside the fenced garden.

Each paling marked on the page
carefully, with a newly-sharpened point.

My sky always pale turquoise.
Invisible hands hold up the sun.

Answer the Door

I don't want to
I look at the cream paint on the front door where it's chipped
Wood shows through
The glass at the top rattles in the wind
I'm too small to see through it
My heart's beating fast
I'm not crying
Knock knock knock knock
Behind me the kitchen door's shut
That's where Mam is
Answer the door
Tell those girls there is no party
I look at the ceiling painted white,
brown marks from dead summer flies around the lightbulb
Knock knock knock knock
I want a party. I want a cake with nine candles. I want a present wrapped with bought paper and golden ribbon that takes a long time to untie.

Party circa 1966

There's me wearing red satin, lace-
collar, cream platform-soled shoes,
listening to, 'You Can't Hurry Love'.

While I've been away, the room's
rearranged itself. Dad's rocking
chair's moved from by the window.

I don't recognise the show on the tele.
The wallpaper Mam loved—
roses over the fireplace—gone.

Outside, the green wooden gate swings
loose on rusty hinges.
Ragged marguerites clump
                    huddle together for warmth.

In the Photograph,
My Mother Wears a Shirtwaister

And here is my mother at the sea-side
smiling with blue eyes, black curly hair,

white earrings matching the white buttons
on the bodice of her shirtwaister.

Lips reddened. I can see the lipstick
even though the photograph is black

and white, like the stripes on her dress
evenly spaced, regular, immoveable.

Bars of a cage. Sharp summer
light streams into the photograph

holding her tight, tight as the heavy
wide belt buckled at her waist.

Rearranging the Furniture

My mother feels the need for change
moving furniture in the front room
whitewashing the ceiling, stripping

old wallpaper and pasting roses
over the fireplace. She shifts
Dad's rocking chair. Now

it's by the fireplace. My mother
replaces lace curtains with a blind,
slats half-opened onto the street.

My mother tries to settle
in that small room,
which is her life.

Tent

It is a very old tent.
Ex-army, khaki, shabby, patched to cover rips and tears.
We take it to the beach with us every summer of my childhood.
It's where we go to change in and out of our bathers—girls first,
eat egg sandwiches gritted with hard sand, drink
hot sweet tea, tasting of metal from a tartan flask,
smell the linseed oil Dad uses to stop the tent cracking
and splitting when it's stored away for winter.

Inside it's like being underwater, clammy, murky.
We hear wind picking up and waves breaking.
The tide's coming in, soon we'll have to pack,
leave for home, but inside the tent we are a family
gathered together after the jumping in and out of the cold North Sea,
warm in our woolly jumpers and everyday clothes.
No longer noisy. Settled. Safe.

The tent our cave and the khaki walls
a screen for the dim light that enters and goes.
Inside the tent we are shadows.

Deserter

Mrs O' Connor next door is Scottish and brings Lucozade when I lie on the sofa, mouth sore after a visit to the dentist. Other times, she plays our piano banging at the keys and when she goes home, Dad plays 'Scotland the Brave'.

One night, she comes knocking at our door, nose bleeding, wrapped in a towel. Her eyes red and blue. Mr O'Connor is in our attic, running across the rafters from their house to ours.

I look out the window to see men wearing red caps running from a jeep.

Dad puts us in the front room and closes the door so we can't see what happens, but I hear them rush up the stairs in one big clatter and then I hear their boots scraping on each step as they bring Mr O' Connor down. I look out the side window and see soldiers dragging him past the privet hedge.

Dad says, he deserves a good hiding and putting in the glass house.

Mam has to swill the front steps and scrub the stair carpet to get rid of his blood.

I Dream My Father

Freshly washed and shaved—
smelling of *Imperial Leather*.
He tips lotion out of the glass bottle,
into big red hands curved into a cup,
slaps it on winter white cheeks.

Wincing at the sting, he says, 'A pity
The Lido's long gone.
Or we'd go there and sit side by side.
Our backs against the warm tiles.
Quiet. Watching the North Sea—
waiting for the tide to turn.'

You're Never Far Away

You come home looking prosperous
like a business man who's been on a long trip,
wearing a never before seen herringbone suit and trilby hat.

I press my face to your newly-shaven cheek,
know it's really you when I smell, *Imperial Leather*.
I've been away,

that's all you say.
I grab your suitcase
                        swing it high.

Glimpse

Lace nets my seven-year-old face
A quick genuflect & blessing

my veil lifts
someone takes my photograph

I watch a sparrow off to the side
about to take flight

or my future
a heavy suitcase packed

with the weight of every soft,
precious thing

The Intellectual

She told herself he was an intellectual. The night they met instead of dancing, he asked her to help him do the crossword. He didn't believe in God. She'd never met anyone who'd said that out loud. Her old headmaster shook his walking stick at him for arguing against the church's teachings. One of her schoolfriends told her she was lucky to know him.

At her house, arguments were discouraged for fear they'd end in shouting matches but in his they all gave their opinions. Even the old grandfather had one. It went on and on. His mother didn't take part. She was in the kitchen cooking. Warming dinner plates on the oven rack. Dishing up each vegetable into a separate tureen and finding serving spoons for soup and dessert. They ate every meal in the dining room. His mother set the table with a cloth and table mats. Even for breakfast.

After a term away at university, he came into the library where she worked, unshaven with the beginnings of a beard and wearing a duffel coat. To tell the truth, she didn't like the scruffy look. Neither did his mother or father and soon, he was clean-shaven again, wearing a white shirt. He borrowed his father's car and drove her out of town to pubs in the country. They had names like 'The Black Swan' or 'The Yorkshire Dragoon.' She drank 'Babycham' and ate ham with pineapple. He preferred beer with ham and eggs.

They read *Lord of the Rings*. Went to concerts. Even the ballet. He told her the world was a safer place than it had ever been though we were having a Cold War. He was an optimist. A man of science. He believed in it. She couldn't go that far. Her family were pessimists. Maybe their Irish DNA. She never read science fiction.

He told her the gold in the ring he gave her came from outer space from inside a supernova and that every human being had gold in their bodies. Even in their toe-nails.

Her mother and father didn't know what to make of him.

She couldn't say, 'No' to him.

Untitled

I've put on my white satin wedding shoes,
I'm ready except my father says,

he won't take me to church,
until I answer this question,

Do you really want to marry this boy?
His very serious face—

he's not much of a joker.
He doesn't want
               to give me away.

War Coat

My father's coat hangs on a peg
in the hallway. Rigid. Khaki.
Brass buttons cold to the touch,
embossed with regimental insignia.
Made by the tailor for a taller,
better-fed man. My father is slight,
underweight, tired after six
long years of battles. Home
this winter night, carrying his war
coat to warm me, in my bed.
When he covers me with his coat,
I feel the weight of sand
                    of desert lonely.

Ice House

In my winter bedroom, snow flowers
bloom on the frozen pane. Tonight's
hot water bottle wrapped in drowsy dreams.

Matthew Mark Luke and John
Bless the bed that I lie on

Dad covers me with his khaki greatcoat
to keep me warm. Medals unpinned. Three
cold stars from India, Africa, Italy.

The Empire Medal and all the others
dropped in a drawer with rusty nails,
twisted screws, broken files.

Good night. Sleep tight.
Mind the bugs don't bite!

Afterword

Doggerland, a land mass, once fertile and populated, that connected Britain to Europe then disappeared beneath the North Sea about 8,000 years ago. It's a lost world but in the winter of 2017/18 it was clearly visible again on the sandy stretch of beach in Redcar, a town in the North East of England, a few miles away from Middlesbrough where I was born and grew up. This phenomenon struck me as a metaphor for how my memory works bringing to the surface: images, glimpses, stories, people and places appearing and disappearing in no set chronology. My memories are random. The immediacy of the child's voice comes and goes co-existing with the voice of the reflective, older self. They move around together in the space of this collection of poems, *Doggerland*.

This is how I remember. Something, usually a sensory experience, triggers a movement and return to my post World War Two childhood growing up in a Northern industrial town at a time of full employment. A settled community of mostly traditional large families—fathers at work and mothers in the home raising children. There's a set order and the adult world of authority: father, mother, teacher, priest, etc who come in and out of the memoir is perceived as 'other', sensed, witnessed and almost never questioned or challenged.

Very little of the big world 'out there' is present in a concrete way but evident in the feeling of unease and need to be safe. The events of the history of the period are mostly absent. It is a small, domestic world imbued with ritual, the seasons, family dynamics, the street, the park, church and school. These are sites of great resonance. They occur and recur. Potent. Emotive. Compelling.

The lived once experience becomes memory afterwards by evocation of my senses. The trigger may be a chant, a rhyme in this very oral community, a touch as in the sting of cold weather especially snow, or the feel of fine fabric or rough khaki. The smell of sea air, shaving lotion or scent. A dream. The sight of a photograph, or a suitcase. The triggers many and varied.

My mother and father ebb and flow in this memoir, particularly my father.

Doggerland is my memory. Particular. Singular. Almost certainly unreliable.

Notes

'Egging': 'egging' is a dialect word.

'Wintering': this is an edited/abridged form of an earlier published poem '76 Birkhall Road'.

'Lost Souls': On All Souls' Day an indulgence for the faithful departed to free them from Purgatory and grant them eternal rest can be granted by devoutly visiting a church or an oratory and reciting an Our Father and the Creed. *Enchiridion of Indulgences*, 1999.

'This Is What Happens': 'They were more likely to go with a woman on her own than a man on his own' Myra Hindley Moors Murderer, Manchester 1963-1965.

'He Can Dance and He Can Sing': Tommy Rhattigan escaped the Moors Murderers. See https://www.youtube.com/watch?v=UoUiaqmoZFk

'Murder by Person or Persons Unknown': Mary Cooper aged 8 ½ years murdered in Albert Park Middlesbrough, June 23 1884 by person or persons unknown. See https://www.thefreelibrary.com/Park%27s+dark+secret.-a0112488175

'I Dream My Father': The Lido Open Air Swimming Pool, Hartlepool was damaged during a great storm in 1953 and all of its structures are now returned to the North Sea.

'Everything Feels Right' previously published as 'Fishpond'

She Can['t] Play the Violin previously published as 'The Girl who disappeared and then came back'

'I feel you breathing' adapted from a short story that won the Adult Section of The Elizabeth Bishop Centenary Writing Competition Nova Scotia in 2011

Acknowledgements

Thanks to the editors of the following venues where some of these poems first appeared:

Blue Nib, Canberra Times, Cicerone, Fem Asia, London Grip, Meniscus, Not very Quiet, University of Canberra Vice-Chancellor's Poetry Prize 2019 Anthology 'Silence'.

'This Is What Happens' was longlisted for the University of Canberra Vice-Chancellor's Poetry Prize 2019

Firstly, a very big thank you to Shane Strange publisher at Recent Work Press who believed in these poems and encouraged me to keep going with the collection. He is a lover of poetry, a generous man and a great asset to the poetry community in Australia and beyond.

My grateful thanks to the following:

Paul Munden who read a small selection of the poems very early on and gave me his time and generous feedback.

Martin Dolan who, as first reader of *Doggerland*, gave much helpful advice.

My fellow workshop poets: Sandra Renew, Sue Peachey, Hazel Hall, Kerrie Nelson and Rosa O'Kane who read and helped shape many of the poems in the collection.

My brother, Peter Brady, who first made me aware of the phenomenon of Doggerland which gave the collection a name and a focus.

Jonathan Brady, my nephew, who told me some stories that became poems.

My brother, John Brady, for the illustration which inspired my poem, 'The Tent'.

Suzanne Edgar who has been, over the years, a constant poetry pal and a source of generous encouragement to me and my poetry.

To the Canberra Community of poets especially @ That Poetry Thing @ Smiths and to Beth and Nigel @Smiths Alternative for providing a venue to read some of these poems.

Finally, to Brian who's been with me and my poetry from the beginning.

About the Author

Moya Pacey was born and grew up in Middlesbrough in the north of England. She came to Canberra in 1978 when it was a country town masquerading as a city and taught English until she retired.

Her poems have won prizes, been read on radio, appeared on buses, gallery walls and published in print and on-line in Australia and overseas.

Doggerland is her third collection. Her previous two poetry collections: *Black Tulips* (Recent Work Press 2017) and *The Wardrobe* (Ginninderra Press 2010) were shortlisted for the ACT Writers Centre Poetry Award. *One Last Border: Refugee Poems* published in 2015 by Ginninderra Press was co-written with Sandra Renew and Hazel Hall.

She is a founding editor of the women's on-line poetry journal *Not Very Quiet* and was awarded, with Sandra Renew, a Canberra Critics' Circle Award in 2019 for her influential work in bringing women's poetry to view via the journal.

In October 2018, she was the Poet in Residence at the Elizabeth Bishop House in Great Village, Nova Scotia, Canada.

She has an MA in Creative and Life Writing from Goldsmiths College, University of London.

www.ingramcontent.com/pod-product-compliance
Lightning Source LLC
Chambersburg PA
CBHW020330010526
44107CB00054B/2059